Cambridge assignments in

GENERAL EDITOR: ROY BENNETT

PERFORMING AND RESPONDING

JOHN HOWARD

Cambridge assignments in

CAMBRIDGE
UNIVERSITY PRESS

Published by the Press Syndicate of the University of Cambridge
The Pitt Building, Trumpington Street, Cambridge CB2 1RP
40 West 20th Street, New York, NY 10011-4211, USA
10 Stamford Road, Oakleigh, Melbourne 3166, Australia

© Cambridge University Press 1995

First published 1995

Printed and bound in Great Britain by
Scotprint Ltd., Musselburgh

A catalogue record for this book is available from the British
Library

ISBN 0 521 422299 paperback.

A compact disc accompanies this book and is available
separately: ISBN 0 521 422302 CD

Author's acknowledgements
I could not have written this book or these pieces without the help
of many people. My particular thanks to: Roy Bennett, Annie
Cave, Peter Nickol, Andy Smith, David Ward, Steve Lowe,
Clifford Lennon and the pupils of Hollyfield School, Surbiton,
and my students at Kingston University.

Acknowledgements
The author and publishers would also like to thank the following
for permission to reproduce photographs and other illustrative
items:
    p. 11 © cliché Bibliothèque Nationale de France, Paris;
    p. 21 © The Hulton Deutsch Collection;
    p. 32 Paul Klee - Stiftung, Kunstmuseum, Bern;
    p. 49 © La Belle Aurore. Steve Davey and Juliet Coombe.

Every effort has been made to reach copyright holders; the
publishers would be glad to hear from anyone whose rights they
may have unknowingly infringed.

Contents

Introduction

for teachers and students

This book contains twelve projects, each with a main theme conveyed in the project title. Each project is based on a piece chosen for listening, and also includes a score of a piece for performing.

I have composed the performance pieces – which are designed for class use – as a response to the listening ones. For this reason they share characteristics in a variety of ways. But in no sense are the performance pieces transcriptions or replacements for the listening pieces. The intention is that they will provide a route towards meaningful listening and analysis, as well as being a musical experience in their own right.

All the projects share the same framework, corresponding to the same basic stages of work:

1 The score of the performance piece, followed by performing directions and advice – Learn, rehearse, perform.

2 Analysis and connections – This is always organised into three sections – the performance piece, the listening piece, and connections between them – and is a chance to explore and discuss the construction of both pieces, and the things they have in common.

3 Listening – Supporting information about the listening piece.

4 Responding – Suggestions for response activities – a chance for pupils to carry out some work of their own: composing, improvising, further listening.

The actual timing of the experience of listening is left to the discretion of the individual teacher. It may, for instance, be appropriate to listen at stage 2 or stage 3, and perhaps to re-listen at the response stage.

Through working with the performance pieces, pupils can be encouraged to respond with musical intelligence to the listening pieces. This approach can be an effective way of breaking down prejudices against 'classical' music. The teacher can make analytical connections between the performance piece and the listening piece, and through such analysis the pupils will become aware of the workings of both pieces. The approach throughout this work should be a creative and enquiring one, with an emphasis on guided and informed discovery.

The listening pieces have been chosen with an emphasis on twentieth-century music, though with some counter-balancing coverage of other periods.

The performance pieces are scored for the kind of resources usually available in school, especially percussion and electronic keyboards. But they should be approached flexibly: the number of musicians can be varied to suit your group sizes and needs, and instrumentation can be varied as necessary to arrive at a performance. Some more difficult parts are included, to cater for the more advanced player (whether teacher or pupil), and several of the pieces may be suitable for the involvement of peripatetic instrumental teachers.

The notes which follow the score have two main aims: to help make the notation understandable, and to assist in solving problems of rehearsal and performance.

Some of the performance pieces need a conductor, others do not. The conductor could be a pupil or a teacher, but it is desirable that pupils should gain experience at directing music.

A polished, complete performance may not always be appropriate; a partial performance or a workshop approach can be equally valid. A complete performance might be built up over a period of time.

A CD accompanies this book. It contains, firstly, the listening pieces – though not the Beethoven (Project 1), Bach (Project 3) or Chopin (Project 12), recordings of which are likely to remain widely available. (Better still, the Bach and Chopin pieces could perhaps be demonstrated on the piano.)

The CD also contains sample performances of the performance pieces. These may help to clarify the scores, and should be of interest when compared with your own performances – what was similar, and what was different?

5

Major/Minor

Based on Symphony No. 5 in C minor
by Beethoven (1770–1827)

Beethoven Bits

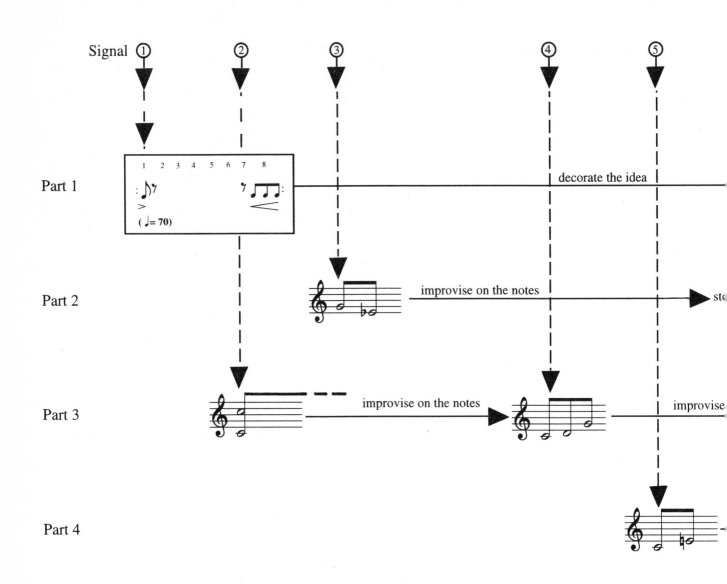

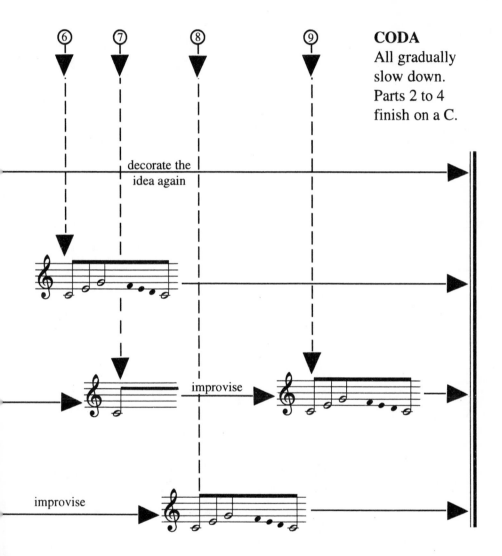

CODA
All gradually
slow down.
Parts 2 to 4
finish on a C.

Performing *Beethoven Bits*

Part 1 is for untuned percussion, parts 2–4 for tuned percussion. Each part can be played by several players. There should also be a conductor, whose main job is to give the numbered signals.

Each horizontal arrow means: keep repeating for the length (duration) of the arrow. Sometimes there is an instruction to 'improvise' or 'decorate'. This means that the players should create music out of the given notes, freely inventing rhythms, or varied ways of playing the instruments. No louds or softs are shown; these should be created by the players according to their idea of the music.

The players of parts 2–4 do not need to keep together, apart from entering and stopping where shown on the score. However, part 1 players *should* basically keep together, counting the 8-beat pattern shown in the boxed rhythm, and maintaining a steady beat throughout the piece.

For part 1 players, the instruction at signals 4 and 7 to 'decorate the idea' means: add more notes to the rhythmic pattern, but preserve the overall 8-beat shape, for instance like this:

Part 1 players can make these decorations individually.

The final tune (parts 2–4, signal 6 onwards) should not be varied in any way apart from the final slowing down. It should be played as three longer notes (C E G) followed by three quick notes (F E D) and a long note C; then repeated. All parts gradually slow down in the coda (signal 9 to the end), with each player in parts 2–4 gradually coming to rest on a long note C.

The conductor must judge the timing of the gaps between signals by listening carefully to the players. The overall length of the piece can therefore vary a great deal – the better the players are at improvising and decorating, the longer the piece can be. It must not be allowed to become dull, with everybody playing medium-loud all the time; it must be exciting and inventive.

Analysis and connections

Beethoven Bits

1 Clap and play part 1's rhythm.

2 The following note-groups are all used in the piece. Combine them to make chords. Play them and listen to them.

Beethoven: Symphony No. 5 in C minor

This symphony is to a large extent based on one main idea or *motif*. This is how the motif appears in the first movement:

It dominates the first movement, and is also important in the symphony's other movements. For instance, here is the theme from the third movement:

Compare the two themes. In fact, the motif occurs in some way or other in each of Beethoven's four movements.

The first movement is organised in a way known as **sonata form**. A first theme (or *subject*) is presented in the main (tonic) key. The music then changes key and a second theme is presented in the new key. If the piece is in a minor key, like this symphony, the second theme is often in the *relative major* (the major key with the same key signature). In this case, C minor is the tonic key, and E♭ major is the relative major. Here is the second theme from the first movement:

Beyond this conflict of keys within the first movement, Beethoven's Fifth Symphony also presents a larger conflict across all four movements. This is a conflict between C minor and C major – a struggle which comes to a head at the end of the third movement. Beethoven then provides a bridge to the fourth movement, where C major triumphs in the shape of this tune:

Connections

There are some close connections between *Beethoven Bits* and Beethoven's Fifth Symphony:

1 The rhythm played by the untuned percussion in *Beethoven Bits* is the same as the rhythm of Beethoven's main motif:

2 *Beethoven Bits* uses the triad of C minor near the beginning, the triad of Beethoven's tonic key.

3 At signals 4 and 5 the music makes use of the idea of conflict (between parts 2, 3 and 4). Beethoven's whole symphony is built on conflict and eventual resolution.

4 In both pieces, the key of C major eventually emerges.

5 The C major tune at the end of *Beethoven Bits* represents agreement, just as in Beethoven's symphony the appearance of C major is often thought of as a symbol of triumph and victory. The tune shared by parts 2–4 near the end of *Beethoven Bits* is related to Beethoven's fourth movement tune (see above). In both pieces the overall structure represents a move from struggle to triumph or agreement.

Of course, in all these comparisons and connections, it is important to remember that our performance piece *Beethoven Bits* is very short, whereas Beethoven's symphony is composed on a large time-scale and uses a full orchestra.

Listening

Beethoven's Fifth Symphony was composed between 1805 and 1808, a period in which he also wrote two other symphonies. It is said to be the first symphony in which trombones were used, and they, along with a piccolo, make a striking contribution when the C major chord appears at the beginning of the fourth movement.

This is quite a long piece of music. Nevertheless, it is good to get a sense of the move from C minor to C major,

and a feel for the structure of the whole piece. Listen at different times to different sections; for instance the following extracts:

- The first movement
- The third movement (scherzo)
- The transition from the end of the third movement into the fourth movement
- The fourth movement

Then, if appropriate, listen to the whole work.

Responding

1 Compose a piece based only on the notes of these two chords:

Build into the piece a sense of conflict between the two chords, perhaps by having a section in which both are used, clashing with one another.

2 Compose or improvise a piece in which one part has a constant rhythmic ostinato and the others use chords and simple tunes.

3 Listen to the slow movement (funeral march) of Beethoven's Symphony No. 3 ('Eroica'). It also has C minor and C major sections. Ask yourself in what ways they contrast with one another.

Palindromes

Based on the first two sections of the rondeau *Ma fin est mon commencement* by Machaut (c.1300–1377)

Forwards & Backwards

metal
percussion
(or equivalent
voices on
keyboards)

Performing *Forwards & Backwards*

This piece is for tuned metal percussion or equivalent voices on electronic keyboards. On percussion, discretion can be used as to which octave the notes are played in. The performance on the *Performing and Responding* CD uses keyboards.

As many players as you wish can play each part, but make sure the parts are roughly balanced. If more than one player takes a part, they must *begin* each bar together, but need not co-ordinate other notes *within* the bar.

Each bar is intended to be about five seconds in duration. It may be helpful to have a conductor who simply marks the start of each bar. Timing *within* each bar is approximate – judged by the performer according to the way the note is positioned in the score. Roughly speaking, bars are divided into two or into three.

The music is played through twice – loudly the first time and softly the second. The bracketed notes are only played the second time through, as a decoration of the main notes. They should be tucked in just before the note they are attached to, and played as fast as possible.

Analysis and connections

Forwards & Backwards

Study the notes of the top line:

Compare them with the notes of the second line:

What is the connection between the two lines?
Now study the notes of the lowest part:

You will discover that it has a sort of mirror shape. The notes of the first half are used in reverse to make the second half, ignoring the decorating notes. This device can be used with letters or numbers; for instance, look at the following:

1991   29.9.92   SOS   redder   minim

The term for this kind of device is **palindrome**.

Machaut: *Ma fin est mon commencement*

There are three parts:

1 The upper part (or *triplum*), played on the CD recording by a tenor recorder.
2 The second part (or *tenor*), sung on the recording.
3 The third part (or *contratenor*), played on the recording by a lute.

The triplum's music is the tenor's music backwards. (Or, equally, the tenor's music is the triplum's music backwards.) The contratenor's section 2 is the same as its first section backwards. In other words, the contratenor, which is half the length of the upper part, must be performed in reverse from the middle of the piece.

Look at the manuscript on the right, which dates from Machaut's time. The lower two staves show the contratenor up to the mid-point; the second half of it is obtained by reading it in reverse. The upper section shows the triplum. To find the tenor part, read backwards from the end (the right hand end of the seventh stave).

Now turn to the next page, where you can see the central section of this music transcribed into modern notation.

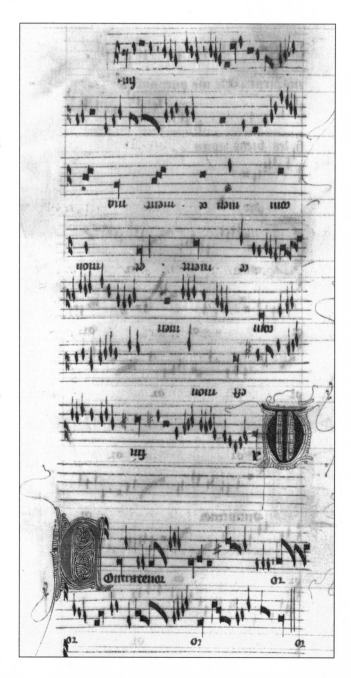

Here is the central part of the recorded extract from
Machaut's *Ma fin est mon commencement*. If you look
carefully, you can see that the tenor's music is the reverse
of the triplum; and that the contratenor mirrors itself at
the mid-point.

One of the main characteristics of this music is the way it cadences. For example, this is the end of the first section:

In 'short score' (suitable for playing on a piano) this would be written like this:

This harmony results from three separate melodic lines, all moving very smoothly – quite different from the way western music was being created three or four hundred years later. The main concern is for melody, as is shown by the top two parts at the beginning:

Connections

1 Both pieces use the same forwards-and-backwards devices: retrograde canon (the same tune going forwards and, in another part, backwards against itself), and palindrome.

2 Both have three melodic lines of music.

3 Both are built from the following scale:

(Note that Machaut uses both F natural and F sharp, depending on the musical context.)

Listening

Guillaume de Machaut was born around 1300 in Champagne in France, lived in Reims, and died in 1377. He was closely associated with the cathedral at Reims, where he was a canon. He is one of the great composers of the medieval period, and was also a poet of substantial skill.

The text of Machaut's piece is really a set of instructions for performance, as well as being a kind of riddle. This project is based on just the first two sections of the rondeau. Here is a translation of their original French text into English:

> My end is my beginning
> And my beginning is my end

As you can see, the words themselves are palindrome-like in their form. Machaut, like other composers of his time, was attracted to the idea of circular structures.

Responding

1 Compose a tune for one instrument, the notes of which turn back on themselves like a palindrome.

2 Listen to the Sanctus and Agnus Dei from Machaut's *Messe de Notre Dame*, listening particularly to the shape of the vocal lines.

3 Compose a short piece for two similar instruments or voices. Design it as a canon, with one voice following the other with the same music, follow-my-leader style.

Invention

Based on Two-part Invention No. 8 in F major
by J. S. Bach (1685–1750)

Four-part Invention

for 4 keyboards (any number of players)

(Choice of voices is left to the players. Use volume control for loud/soft and <>)

each pattern should be
played 3 times before next entry

Keyboards 1-3 cut off

Performing *Four-part Invention*

This piece is written for keyboards, in four parts, but for any number of players to each part as long as they are balanced. Where there is more than one player to a part, it is not necessary to co-ordinate your playing, *except* that you should start each entry together, and co-ordinate the last two bars. You are free to choose the voices to be used on each keyboard.

Here is a key to some of the notation used:

a held note

a group of notes played fairly quickly

repeat the group of notes to the end of the arrow

♩ = 70   the speed should be about 70 crotchets per minute

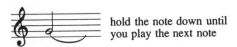
hold the note down until you play the next note

When playing the keyboard parts, find the hand position which can play as much of the music as possible and stick to it, only moving the hand when necessary.

It may be helpful to have a conductor, to bring in the players, beat the ²⁄₄ bars, and give the cut-offs where marked. Alternatively, try letting the players co-ordinate the piece by signalling to each other as appropriate.

Analysis and connections

Four-part Invention

Answer the following questions. They will help you identify what is happening in the piece you have performed.

1 What do parts 1–3 do in the first bar? Describe the effect.

2 What does part 4 do in the first bar? Describe the effect.

3 Can you write out the scale upon which most of this piece is based?

4 There are two notes in the piece which are outside that scale. Can you identify them?

5 Compare the first bar with the second. How are they different?

6 What sort of impression does part 4's note B make in bars 2–3?

7 What about the E♭ in part 3, bars 6–7? What sort of effect does it have?

8 Does the piece sound complete? Have we ended on the right note?

Bach: Two-part Invention in F major

This music contains two melodic lines (tunes) which are closely connected. For instance, they often imitate (echo) each other. The first time this happens is at the beginning, when the upper line begins like this:

The lower line comes in almost immediately with the same music one octave lower:

If we look at this tune, we can see that it is based on two ideas:

and

The first idea is really a chord, with its notes presented one after the other instead of all at once. This is often termed a **broken chord** for obvious reasons. The second idea is made out of the scale of F major.

There is also a third idea:

This idea uses a finger pattern, always has quick notes (semiquavers), and is always based on part of a chord. For instance, the first time it appears it is based on the chord of F:

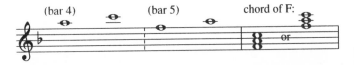

Bach's piece shows how to be truly inventive with these ideas, by playing around with them in different ways and by changing key a number of times. The piece is divided into two sections (this is often known as **binary form**), with the first section ending in C major (the dominant key of F) and the second moving through a number of other keys. Eventually, to create a satisfying ending, the music returns to the key of F.

Connections

If you refer to the answers you gave to the questions on the opposite page, about *Four-part Invention,* you will discover some interesting things:

1 Like the Bach piece, it begins with a broken chord idea in F.

2 This is followed (in the 4th keyboard part) by the use of part of the F scale (at the end of bar 1).

3 Bar 2 includes an idea like Bach's third (finger-pattern) idea.

4 The notes B (bars 2–3) and E♭ (bars 6–7) are not contained in the key and scale of F major. They help to push the music towards different keys. The B pushes it towards the key of C (the dominant of F), and the E♭ towards the key of B♭. Thus we followed roughly the same design as Bach: first section F to C, second section towards B♭, returning to F for the last three bars.

All these things connect *Four-part Invention* to the Bach Invention. But Bach's piece is more extended, works at a faster pace, and covers many more keys.

Listening

The title page of the autograph edition of Bach's Inventions is dated 1723. In the foreword Bach wrote that his intention was 'to teach clear playing in two and three obbligato parts, good inventions [compositional ideas] and a cantabile manner of playing'. His piece is therefore an attempt:

1 to encourage and develop good keyboard playing,

2 to demonstrate some effective compositional ideas,

3 to show that he could make use of them inventively,

4 to help people get a taste for composition.

The recording of the Bach Invention which you listen to may be performed on a piano or perhaps a harpsichord. It is interesting to compare the different effect of these instruments.

Responding

1 Listen to another of Bach's Two-part Inventions and identify some of the musical ideas.

2 Listen to one of his Three-part Inventions (three melodic lines instead of two).

3 Compare piano performances with harpsichord ones. Listen to a clavichord if possible.

4 Compose a piece for two players, using this scale and this chord as the raw material:

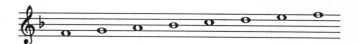

Give each player a melodic line. Try to maintain a consistent musical character throughout the piece, as Bach does in his Inventions, rather than having strong contrasts. You can use *Four-part Invention* as a model.

Vowel Sounds

Based on 'O King', the second movement of the *Sinfonia*
by Luciano Berio (born 1925)

Sang Red

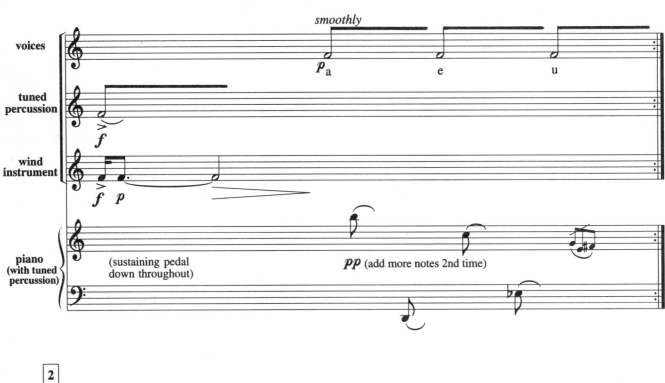

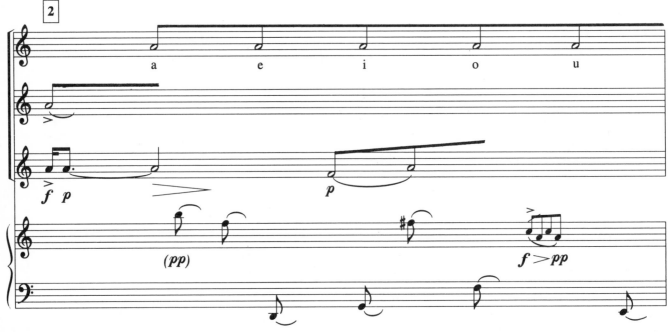

Performing *Sang Red*

The vocal line should be sung slowly, with all voices rhythmically together and with the notes quite long. The instruments – except at the beginning of each bar – take their cue from the voices, following the score to see how to time their notes in relation to the top line. If a conductor is used, his or her role can be limited to marking the first beat of each bar, where the accented rhythm appears in the wind instrument part.

The vocal part may be sung at pitch and/or down an octave. It is a kind of chant, and the vowel sounds should be as follows:

a   as in *sang*
e   as in *red*
i   as in *in*
o   as in *hot*
u   as in *sun*

These words together form the text 'Sang red in hot sun' which gradually unfolds in the vocal line and is sung complete near the end.

The wind instrument part could alternatively be played on a string instrument. In the accented rhythm at the beginning of each bar, the *f* should be clear and the *p* very sudden and much quieter.

For the first tuned percussion part there can be several players, but they should always keep together – with each other and with the wind part.

The piano and second tuned percussion should be very quiet except where a special *f* effect appears. The choice of instruments for the second percussion part will depend on what is available. You can combine instruments that individually can only play some of the notes, and it is possible to change the octave positions if necessary. Nevertheless, the piano should play all the written notes in the correct octaves. Piano and tuned percussionists do not need to keep together except on the *f* effects and the final bar of the piece. Also, piano and wind do not need to co-ordinate exactly, except at the beginnings of bars. The printed notation is therefore an approximate realization of the piece.

In the first bar, the pianist and tuned percussionists can add some extra notes during the repeat if they wish.

Analysis and connections

Sang Red

The vocal line concentrates on the note F at first, then moves to A, and later B. It returns repeatedly to F, but at the end has a twist of direction by moving down through E♭ to finish (a little surprisingly) on D♭. The first tuned percussion part and the wind instrument have the role of signalling the start of each line of the tune, almost always

sharing the same note, and anticipating the note with which the vocal line will start its next phrase. The exception is bar 3, where the percussion part has a B and the wind part an F, which makes the harmony momentarily more coloured. The piano/percussion part acts as a form of colour in the piece, decorating the vocal line, always in the background and very quiet apart from the occasional gesture which begins loud. The last bar of the piece unites all the instruments on a unison F.

Berio: O King

The composer uses a set of seven notes to generate the vocal tune and other parts:

This is taken from two whole-tone areas:

The music is continually disturbed by *sforzando* notes, which actually outline a much slower version of the pitch set. The role of the vibraphone, harp and piano is to add decoration to the voices and other instruments. At the end, the voices fall away to D♭, and continue downward to form an 8-part chord.

The text of the piece is suggested by the title. It gradually permutates the vowels *o*, *a* and *i* (as in *Martin*), and *u* and *e* (as in *Luther*). The vowels are eventually put into the right order, and the consonants added. Finally, the complete phrase is used: 'O Martin Luther King'.

Connections

1 The notes of the tune in *Sang Red* use the first part of the note set used by Berio.

2 In both pieces, the text is broken up at first, gradually changing to form intelligible words near the end.

3 Both pieces use *sforzando* effects.

4 Both use very quiet notes to decorate the vocal tune, covering a wide pitch-range, mainly on the piano.

5 In both, several instruments and voices share the same tune, and the music is controlled and dominated by that tune.

Listening

Berio's *O King* is a meditation on the name Martin Luther King, the American civil rights leader who was shot in 1967. The piece forms the second movement of Berio's *Sinfonia*, completed in 1968, but had previously existed in a smaller-scale version before Berio composed the *Sinfonia*. It is characteristic of this composer that he should create two different versions of the same piece, for he likes to re-work his own (and other people's) music; for instance his *Sequenza VI* for solo viola later became *Chemins II* for viola and orchestra.

The *Sinfonia* is also interesting for its use of voices. It was originally composed for the Swingle Singers, and demands more of a jazz singing style than a concert hall one. Note how the singers mostly sing without vibrato.

Responding

1 Compose a piece in a meditative style – slow, calm and repetitive – for voices and keyboards, using only the following notes:

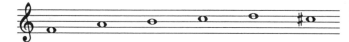

2 Make up your own piece for voices, using a text you have invented out of the vowel sounds. During the piece, gradually construct the text out of the vowels and consonants.

3 For further experience of Berio's vocal writing, listen to *A-Ronne* and *Cries of London*, performed by Swingle II.

Luciano Berio

Hymn and a River

Based on 'The Housatonic at Stockbridge', No. 3 of
Three Places in New England by Charles Ives (1874–1954)

River

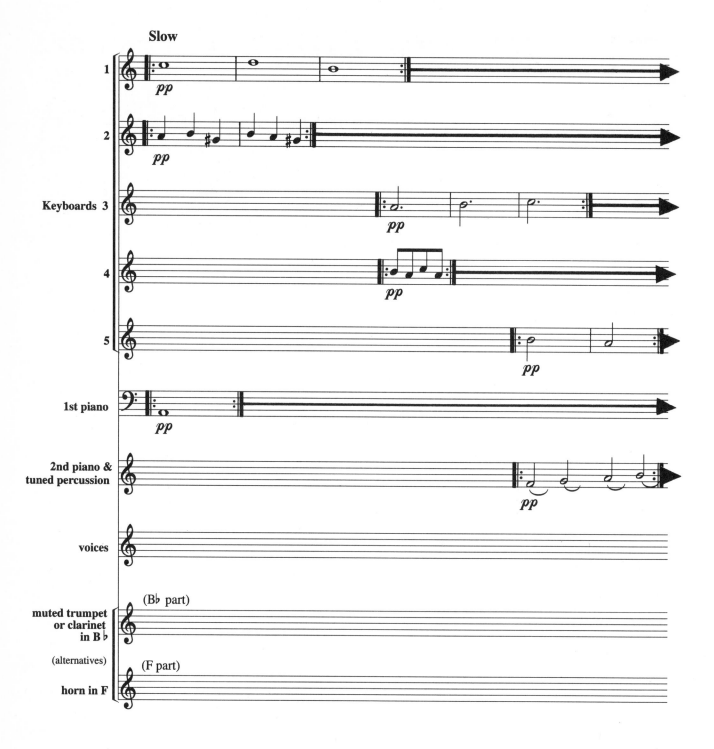

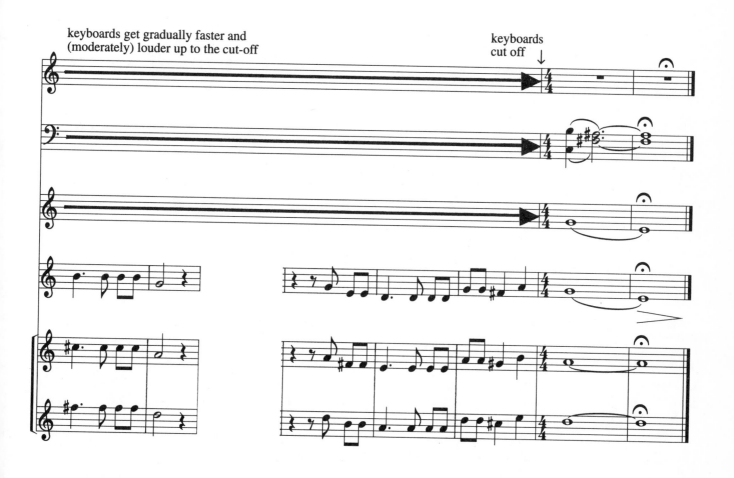

keyboards get gradually faster and (moderately) louder up to the cut-off

keyboards cut off

Performing *River*

River is scored for:
- five electronic keyboards,
- two pianos (the second doubled by tuned percussion) (the two piano parts can be played by two performers at one piano),
- voices (any number),
- clarinet or muted trumpet or horn (a line for horn in F is included in the score).

The piece should be performed at a slow tempo. The keyboard and piano parts have continually repeating material, and this continues without a break until the last two bars. A conductor should:

1 bring in each of the instruments,
2 bring in each of the voice entries,
3 cut off the keyboards near the end,
4 beat 4 during the last but one bar, and give the final cut-off.

The voices and the clarinet/trumpet/horn part should keep absolutely together. They should maintain a moderately slow $\frac{3}{4}$ time, and try to blend in such a way that the voices sound like an instrument. The tune is part of a hymn-tune, entitled *Missionary*:

The keyboard, piano and percussion parts do not need to keep absolutely together. If desired, any of these parts can be played by more than one person; these players only need to be together at entry points and for the last two bars (where *everybody* should be together). It is important that the keyboards, pianos and percussion remain soft, and not overpower the voices and clarinet/trumpet/horn, even in the crescendo near the end.

Analysis and connections

River

The keyboard texture is meant to be rather like a river: different patterns of different lengths combining to make a shifting impression, rather like the moving surface of the water (in a sort of A minor). These patterns are all placed above a constant pedal note A on the piano.

The hymn (in the key of G major) floats through the river music, so that there is a mysterious combination of free-time music and the stricter $\frac{3}{4}$ of the hymn.

The river music gets faster and louder, reaching a

loud climax – which is then followed by a strange ending in which the music sounds somewhat unfinished, partly because of the final chord:

The music sounds as though it will carry on, rather than finish definitely – perhaps just as a river flows on.

Ives: *The Housatonic at Stockbridge*

The Housatonic is a river, and this piece is one of a set of three collectively called *Three Places in New England*.

The music contains the following elements:

1 The piece begins with impressionistic muted string textures, like mist and running water, and these continue for most of the piece. Some of the notated rhythms are very complex, creating a polyrhythmic (many-rhythmed) texture:

2 The harp picks out certain notes, rather like droplets of water. There is further decoration on the celeste.
3 The low strings and an organ play a very low C♯ almost throughout the piece. This is a sort of pedal note which quietly pins together the rest of the music above it.
4 A tune adapted from the hymn-tune *Missionary* is played by horns and cor anglais in the key of D♭ (C♯), so that the low pedal note on strings and organ is the tonic of the tune.

These elements could be imagined as representing the following:

1 The mist and the running water (upper strings, harp, celeste)
2 The singing of a hymn in a church (horns, cor anglais)

The piece meanders along (deliberately) but then rather suddenly comes to life, reaching a loud climax of sound just before the end, with the brass particularly prominent. Here, it has been suggested, Ives is seeing the river differently, with its waters powerfully pushing towards the sea. This loud music is soon cut off, to reveal the distant and quiet string sound underneath – a memory of the river as it was, perhaps. The final chord produces an enigmatic, unresolved ending:

This ending could be thought of as a distant memory of a deeply-felt experience.

Connections

1 Both pieces use the same hymn-tune.
2 Both have an ending which sounds unresolved and unfinished because of the character of the closing harmony.
3 Both attempt to portray in sound an impression of a river, with patches of mist.
4 Both pieces get louder and more animated towards the end.
5 Both use a pedal note.

Listening

'We walked in the meadows along the River, and heard the distant singing from the Church across the River. The mist had not entirely left the river bed, and the colors, the running water, the banks and elm trees were something that one would always remember.'
Charles Ives, after a Sunday morning walk with his wife at Stockbridge, Massachusetts, June 1908

On his return home, Ives sketched some music which, by 1913, had become the orchestral piece *The Housatonic at Stockbridge*. A further inspiration for Ives was a poem of the same title by Robert Underwood Johnson. The poet describes the 'contented river', and at the end – reflected in the build-up of sound and activity near the end of Ives's music – says:

Let me tomorrow thy companion be,
By fall and shallow to the adventurous sea!

It is typical of Ives that he should include a quotation of a tune written by somebody else. He did this in almost every piece that he wrote, using popular tunes, military marches, dance tunes and religious songs. It is also typical of him to have created several versions of the piece, starting in 1908 and 'finishing' in 1913, but with some further work on the orchestration in 1914. A final version was created in 1929, and the first performance took place in New York in 1930. Many of his pieces exist in several versions or even remained unfinished.

Responding

1 Compose a short piece of river music for keyboards, using note-patterns of differing lengths, for example:

Pattern 1

Pattern 2

2 Listen to other pieces by Charles Ives. The vigorous *Robert Browning Overture* (1911) was planned as part of a series about 'Men of Literature' but Ives finished only this one. Its structure is traditional, with slow introduction, allegro, adagio, allegro repeat, and fugal coda. It is only in the final section that Ives indulges his love of quotation, with a striking reference to *Adeste fideles* ('O come, all ye faithful'). Listen also to the second movement of Symphony No. 4 – not so much to identify actual tunes quoted, but more to appreciate the Ivesian mixture of styles that results, including hymns, dance music, popular songs and marches. In the third movement, Ives quotes extensively the hymn 'From Greenland's icy mountains'.

3 Compose a piece using the following hymn-tune as part of the music:

Old Hundredth

You could use it complete, but one phrase at a time (as Ives does). Surround it with other music, above and below it in pitch. Alternatively, you could make your piece out of fragments of the tune. Use it to create your musical ideas.

Fixed Ideas

Based on *Carmen Arcadiae Mechanicae Perpetuum*
by Harrison Birtwistle (born 1934)

Mechanisms

Performing *Mechanisms*

This needs to be performed with precision, in a mechanical style of playing. Apart from the pause bars, the music is deliberately measured and would therefore benefit from having a conductor. The dynamics range from very soft to very loud, moving suddenly and abruptly from one to the other (for instance: bar 4 very loud, bar 5 very soft).

The pause bars – 3, 7 and 20 – should be conducted with two signals: one for the downbeat, the other for the short chord.

Analysis and connections

Mechanisms

There are five 'mechanisms' (or fixed ideas) in this piece, plus the linking pause-bar idea. Each of the mechanisms has its own instrumentation, lending it a unique sound, as follows:

Mechanism 1 – strings and woodwind

Mechanism 2 – piano and electronic keyboard

Mechanism 3 – flute and clarinet

Mechanism 4 – brass

Mechanism 5 – strings

These 'mechanisms' change very little throughout the piece, each retaining its sound and identity. However, each one is used both loud and soft, so that to some extent the plan of dynamics is separate from the plan of ideas.

Birtwistle: *Carmen Arcadiae Mechanicae Perpetuum* ('The perpetual song of mechanical Arcady')

Six musical 'mechanisms' are used in this piece. This, for instance, is the one first played in bar 2:

Those chords, together, make this overall rhythm:

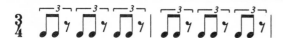

This contrasts with the woodwind and string mechanism which happens after about 33 seconds of the piece:

This mechanism has this overall rhythm:

The way in which these two mechanisms contrast is typical of the piece, and made even more striking because the music is structured so that the mechanisms follow one another without transitions between them. The effect of this is, at times, deliberately abrupt and often dramatic – partly because the louds and softs have a time-scale unrelated to that of the mechanisms. Compare, for instance, the first texture, contained in bars 1–7 (up to the held note on the brass), with its continuation from bar 9. The first time it is loud, the second soft.

This rather random process is also applied to the octave registers within which the ideas occur. Compare this brass idea which occurs after about 1³/₄ minutes

with the related low-pitched texture which takes place

after 2 minutes 34 seconds. (In practice this is difficult to hear. Listen for the bass trombone playing F – G♯ in very loud quavers; this doubles the F and G♯ in the bass clarinet.)

It is as though the composer has three separate schemes running through the piece – one for the order of the mechanisms, the second for louds and softs, the third for registers.

Another aspect of this piece is its dramatic nature. Birtwistle has often written semi-theatrical music, in which the instruments almost take on the roles of characters in an unseen drama. *Carmen Arcadiae Mechanicae Perpetuum* has the feel of a drama, an interplay between musical ideas and an interplay between instruments and families of instruments – although of course there is no plot, nothing written down apart from the musical text. We are free to respond for ourselves.

Listen particularly to the held notes in the piece. This idea is transformed into a sort of climax near the end, when all the instruments participate. Also listen to the dance-like quality of the very beginning, and the rather earthy feel at the end. This is how the composer notates the end:

It is unusual to find an ending on a sustained note with the instruction 'molto rall' above it. Since a held note cannot slow down by itself, there is the suggestion here of a composer's joke, for he could have written a pause over the note to obtain the same aural effect. On the other hand, Birtwistle has long been interested in the theatrical ritual of music-making, and may be signalling the close of this particular piece's ritual interplay with a visual pulse (the conductor's beat) rather than an aural one.

The piece is scored for flute (doubling piccolo), oboe, clarinet (doubling bass clarinet), bassoon (doubling double bassoon), trumpet, horn, trombone, marimba, piano or electric piano, 2 violins, viola, cello and double bass.

Connections

1 Both pieces use 'mechanisms' (ideas unchanging in pitch and rhythm) which create rather extreme contrasts.

2 Both use a separate scheme for dynamics (although Birtwistle's is much more thoroughgoing than the one in *Mechanisms*).

3 Although the instrumentation is different, both pieces use the sound of a mixed chamber-sized ensemble.

Listening

Carmen Arcadiae Mechanicae Perpetuum was composed in 1977 for the tenth birthday of the London Sinfonietta, who gave the first performance the following year.

The title means 'The perpetual song of mechanical Arcady'. The piece is a kind of homage to the painter Paul Klee (indeed, the title is the sort of title Klee might have used), and relates to Klee's picture *The Twittering Machine*, which shows four mechanical birds. Instead of the birds, Birtwistle has six musical ideas or mechanisms.

Responding

1 Create a piece out of three mechanical ideas, which may be rhythms only, or perhaps played on just one or two notes each. For example:

If you use (pitched) notes, experiment with the effect of moving ideas between different octave registers.

2 Form a group of musicians with a variety of instruments/voices. Improvise a piece using just a few simple textures (for instance, everybody using low-pitched sounds). Once you have devised and tried out your textures, impose a separate scheme of louds and softs so that each texture appears at least twice, once loud and once soft.

3 Listen if possible to other pieces by Birtwistle. *Verses for Ensembles* is an interesting example of the composer's use of theatre and spacing. Each wind player has several positions from which to play, and the movement of the musicians during the piece is part of the theatre. *Earth Dances* is an energetic orchestral piece, bursting with strong musical ideas and fascinating contrasts. It possesses the characteristic Birtwistle feeling of the enactment of a ritual. *Endless Parade* is an exciting concerto for trumpet and orchestra, inspired by a carnival procession.

Paul Klee (1879-1940), *Konzert auf dem Zweig* (Recital on the Branch), 1921, a version of *The Twittering Machine*

New/Old

Based on 'Bonnie James Campbell' from
Scotch Minstrelsy by Judith Weir (born 1954)

Ballad

Performing *Ballad*

Ballad is scored for synthesiser or wind instrument (or any suitable substitute), tuned metal percussion, tuned wooden percussion, two woodblocks and two drums. The main tune should have one player, but the percussion parts may be doubled by several players, being careful nevertheless not to cover up the tune.

A conductor is not essential, but may help to keep a tight ensemble. The dynamics and articulation should be observed as accurately as possible. The character of the music should be one of suppressed violence, in keeping with the original ballad text.

Analysis and connections

Ballad

This has a short introduction leading to three verses, and a short coda. The tune remains the same for each verse, but the amount of percussion is gradually increased so that the sound becomes louder and more complex.

The tune is modal, based on the following scale:

The percussion music is constructed as a series of repeating patterns, contrasting with the broader sense of line and contour in the tune. A further (but related) contrast is between the apparent simplicity and innocence of the tune, and the somewhat harder edge of the percussion accompaniment.

Judith Weir: *Bonnie James Campbell*

Here is the text of the song:

> It's up in the highlands, along the sweet Tay,
> Bonnie James Campbell rode many a day.
> He saddled, he bridled and gallant rode he,
> And home came his good horse but never came he.
>
> Out came his old mother a-crying full sair,
> Out came his bonnie bride tearing her hair.
> 'My meadow lies green and my corn is unshorn,
> But Bonnie James Campbell will never return.'
>
> Saddled and bridled and booted rode he,
> A plume in his helmet, a sword at his knee.
> Empty his saddle all bloody to see;
> Oh home came his good horse but never came he.

Like many such poetic ballads, this combines a simple rhyming scheme and lilting rhythm with an atmosphere of violence – a violence which is slightly under the surface, but perhaps more ominous as a result. In her music, Judith Weir exploits this to the full, using the piano to comment on the voice and giving the singer a line which is fundamentally simple in its shape, especially at the beginning, but which threatens to break out of that simplicity. Here is an example of the tenor line from the first verse:

Compare this with the beginning of the third verse. The basis of the line remains the same, but it has now become varied and more expressive:

Here is a brief description of the music of each verse, to help you to follow the growing drama of the piece:

Verse 1 – a very simple piano accompaniment made up of long notes, doubling some of the notes of the voice and helping to emphasise important words.

Verse 2 – the piano has staccato figures, descending in pitch. There is a strong atmosphere of suppressed violence, enhanced by the rhythms in the piano, and an element of surprise on the final 'return'.

Verse 3 – a more elaborate accompaniment made out of falling scales, with an effect of acceleration, becoming tremolo effects; then a triplet figure, alternating the right hand and left hand. Again, a feeling of violence in the *sff* single notes. The piece is rounded off by the alternating figure, giving a feeling of understatement at the end.

Connections

1 Both pieces have a tune and an accompaniment, and in both the accompaniment grows in weight and complexity from verse to verse.

2 In both pieces the accompaniment is based on

repeated patterns used rather strictly – contrasting with the greater flexibility of rhythm and pitch of the solo tune.

3 Both pieces are based on the same tune – though *Ballad* uses a relatively simple version. Compare the first verse of each:

Weir: *Bonnie James Campbell*

Ballad

Listening

'Bonnie James Campbell' is one song from a cycle (or collection) of five, entitled *Scotch Minstrelsy*, written in 1982. The composer writes about the work: '*Scotch Minstrelsy* is a song cycle comprising settings of five (greatly abbreviated) Scottish ballads whose subject matter is almost exclusively violent happenings which take place against the beautiful background of the Scottish countryside. It was my intention to reflect this underlying irony in the way the words are set to music.'

In each of the songs in the cycle, the composer exploits this contrast of beauty and savagery. It is interesting that she has chosen to set them with just piano accompaniment, rather than choosing large forces (e.g. orchestra) to convey the violence. We do not have to use loud and powerful sounds in order to express powerful ideas. Another reason is that the feeling of restraint resulting from using piano helps the composer to convey the underlying, somewhat hidden, violence of the situations described in the words.

Responding

1 Compose a tune for the words of 'Bonnie James Campbell'. Add some accompanying music, either for keyboard or for a small group of percussion instruments. Construct the accompaniment out of repeating patterns, with new ones entering for each successive verse. Compose an ending which matches the character of the text.

2 Listen to other works by Judith Weir. *King Harald's Saga* is most interesting because it has one soprano singer enacting all the roles in a kind of mini-opera.

There is virtuosic use of different vocal styles and registers to articulate the difference between the characters. *Missa del Cid* (1988) is a music drama which combines two texts: a thirteenth-century Spanish poem describing a bloody crusade, and parts of the Latin Mass. It is typical of Judith Weir's ironic approach that the words of the latter are allowed to comment on the former.

3 Create a piece of music and drama based on the story of Bonnie James Campbell. This could either be a large project or one which is improvised quite quickly. Use some of the following ideas:

- Have a small band of musicians create music which comments on the action of the drama at appropriate points (perhaps between each verse of the story); have the actors freeze while these sections of music are being played.
- Use a narrator to tell the story.
- Create a short section of music corresponding to each of the characters in the story. Then make a musical structure out of them, which can be played while the action is mimed. Try to avoid just 'sound effects'; aim to create a structure out of the musical ideas. A good test of whether it works well as music is to perform it alone, without the action. Decide from your listening whether you feel the music has a character of its own.

Loops and Shakes

Based on 'Shaking and Trembling', the first movement of
Shaker Loops by John Adams (born 1947)

Loops

Performing *Loops*

Loops is scored for five electronic keyboards, although it may be performed on any group of suitably-pitched and well balanced instruments. It will work with several instruments to each part.

The choice of keyboard voice-settings may be made by the players. However, it is important that each sound is clearly different from the others, so that each pattern (or loop) can be heard clearly, and without any one pattern dominating.

Dynamic levels are also left to the players' judgement. Several options would make sense in this piece: for instance, the whole thing could be done as a gradual crescendo; or as a gradual diminuendo; or with each player working out a distinctive pattern of louds and softs for their own part. You can compare two different performances of the piece on the CD, each with a different plan of dynamics.

The music should be played as fast as possible but also as *accurately* as possible – not so fast that it becomes out of control. There should be no slowing down at the end. The tempo and metre are the same for all the parts; there is no free time.

Analysis and connections

Loops

The title describes the repeating patterns contained in the piece. Each part has its own loop. Part 1's loop lasts 8 beats, part 2's 6 beats, part 3's 5 beats, part 4's 7 beats and part 5's 5 beats.

They all start at different times, but once started keep repeating until near the end. Here, each pattern, led by part 5, is gradually altered so that it ends on the note B. The final sound of the piece is therefore a unison B.

John Adams: *Shaker Loops*

The first section of Adams's piece is called 'Shaking and Trembling', and the music is made out of repeating patterns or loops. The term 'loops' connects with a technique used by composers of electronic music, in which sounds are recorded onto continuous loops of tape, and then textures created by combining several tape-loops. (This way of creating overlapping repeated patterns has now been largely superseded by digital techniques using sequencers.)

There are two kinds of loops in Adams's piece:

1 Those made up of groups of quick notes:

2 Those with long notes:

The music is written in precise notation, without use of free- or space-time notation within the individual instrumental parts. However, there is quite a lot of freedom concerning how the parts combine, and how many times a loop is repeated.

The music is organised in nine sections. Each section is based on a particular scale, and the following plan sets out in an approximate form the scheme of keys and durations:

Section 1	long	E minor / G major
Section 2	long	F major
Section 3	quite long	B♭ minor / D♭ major
Section 4	very short	B♭ major
Section 5	quite long	C major
Section 6	quite short	G minor / B♭ major
Section 7	very short	E minor / G major
Section 8	very short	F♯ minor
Section 9	quite short	B♭ minor / D♭ major

As you listen, notice the change of key and mood which happens as section 2 begins. The way the music grows through each section, changing a little at a time, is crucial to this style.

In several sections the scale used is not quite major and not quite minor, which is why the plan above shows them in alternative forms. For instance, in section 1 the scale is:

This is one of the older forms of scale known as **modes**; this one is the Aeolian Mode, which has a minor third between the first and third notes and a whole tone between the seventh and eighth notes. Much of Adams's piece uses modes rather than major or minor scales.

Connections

1 Both pieces use repeating loops of music.
2 Both organise pitches within a sense of scale or mode. *Loops* uses just one mode, outlining the scale C B A G F E D C, mostly in descending order. Adams's piece, of course, changes mode from section to section.
3 Both pieces explore the way patterns interact in time, even though *Loops* stays within $\frac{3}{4}$ time while *Shaking and Trembling* is more complex.
4 Both start by bringing in the parts one by one.
5 Both start with a fairly high-pitched part and gradually introduce lower ones. *Shaking and Trembling* covers a much wider pitch-range than *Loops*; listen for the entry of the double bass.

Listening

Shaker Loops was written in 1978. The title refers to the Shakers, a virtually extinct American religious sect who used to shake and tremble during their worship, dancing and singing, using wild gestures and exaggerated melodic phrases. Originally the Shakers came from England, settling in the United States after 1774. They are connected to the Quakers.

The title also refers to musical shaking or trilling, where two adjacent notes are rapidly alternated.

The 'loops' are repeating tunes or fragments, each of a different length. When combined, these create the impression that the music is always changing.

Shaker Loops is in four movements, called 'Shaking and Trembling', 'Hymning Slews' (a slew is a slide between two notes), 'Loops and Verses' and 'A Final Shaking'. The composer skilfully makes each movement merge into the next, by use of overlaps, so that the whole piece plays continuously from start to finish. (The CD which goes with this book, however, contains only the first movement, 'Shaking and Trembling'.)

Responding

1 Listen to other pieces by John Adams: *The Chairman Dances* (foxtrot for orchestra), *Fearful Symmetries* or *The Wound-dresser.*
2 Adams – to an extent, at least – belongs to a group of composers known as **minimalists**, although *Shaker Loops* is not particularly representative of the style called minimalism. The minimalist composers make use of simple patterns and ideas, often creating interesting effects by making patterns move in and out of phase. For another perspective on pattern-making in music, listen to some of the music of other minimalist composers: Steve Reich, Terry Riley, Michael Nyman and Philip Glass.
3 Parts of *Shaking and Trembling* can be compared with parts of *The Rite of Spring* by Stravinsky, although Stravinsky's techniques and ways of notating his music are rather different. Listen to the 'Dance of the Earth' at the end of Part 1 of *The Rite of Spring*.
4 Create your own loop piece for several players. Each player creates their own looping pattern for use in the piece, then the group decides how these loops should be combined.
5 Improvise a piece for three players that starts on a unison note shared by all three, and returns to it at the end.
6 Imagine that *Loops* is the first section of a longer piece. Compose the music of a second section, using a different key.
7 Create a large rondo structure – A B A C A D A – in which *Loops* forms the A section. New sections are composed for B, C and D; each could be composed by a different group of musicians. Give a complete performance.

Moonlight and a River

Based on *Moonlight on a Spring River*
(Chinese traditional tune, ensemble version)

Light on the Water

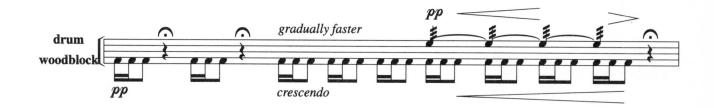

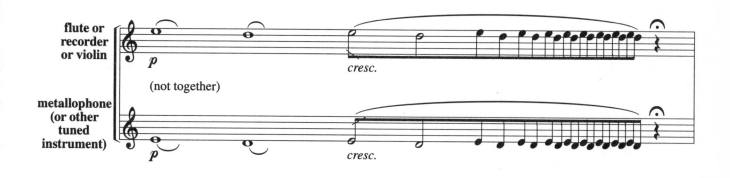

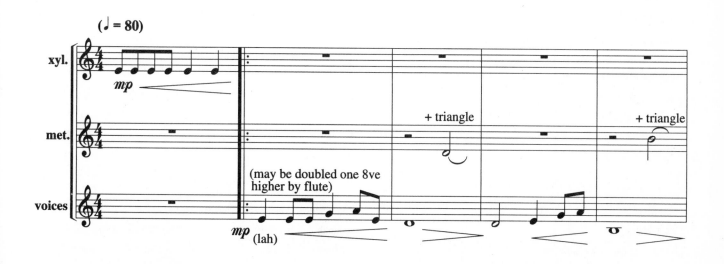

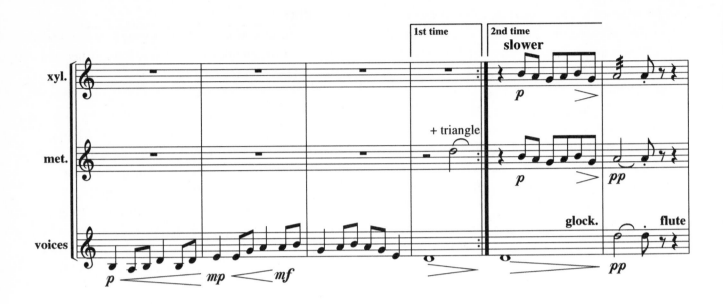

Performing *Light on the Water*

The introduction and coda should be played freely. The main section is in 4/4 time, slowing down in the last two bars. If a conductor is used, it should be to set the 4/4 tempo and conduct the main section, leaving the introduction and coda to the players.

The vocal line, which can be doubled if necessary by the flute, should be sung to 'lah'. The voices are really functioning as instruments. If desired, the line can be sung both at the written pitch and an octave below.

Dynamics should be observed as closely as possible, and the music performed expressively.

Analysis and connections

Light on the Water

The design is simple and straightforward. A short, rather free introduction, using first percussion, then a wind instrument, leads to a main section. This is begun by a xylophone, preparing the $\frac{4}{4}$ time before the tune itself enters. This is sung in unison, in simple $\frac{4}{4}$ time, with just a touch of colour from a metallophone and triangle at the end of each phrase, and the use of a slower figure on xylophone and metallophone to mark the final cadence of the tune. The flute then completes the piece with a free coda, and there is a final touch of colour from the glockenspiel (echoing the end of the middle section).

The tune is based on the following scale:

This is made out of a pentatonic (five-note) scale, with an added F♯.

Moonlight on a Spring River (traditional Chinese tune)

This piece is in several sections. (Our performance piece, *Light on the Water*, is based on the first section only.) It is long, and alternates passages for the *pipa* (a type of lute) with orchestral sections. These consist of a unison tune which is shared by the whole ensemble – there is no real harmony as such, for the interest in the music lies in the line of the tune itself, and the mixture of colours used in the ensemble to play it. The ending of almost every section achieves a sense of rest with the use of high harmonics. In the last section, after the activity of previous sections, the music reaches a peaceful resolution. The piece ends with a coda.

Connections

1 The melodies are very closely connected, *Light on the Water* being based on part of *Moonlight on a Spring River*.

2 Both have an introduction in free time, featuring the same rhythm (on drum or lute), accelerating figures, and a two-note tremolando.

3 They share a characteristic cadence figure, using a harmonic in the Chinese piece and the glockenspiel in *Light on the Water*:

4 Both have a unison tune, mostly without harmony, and in a simple metre.

5 Both are based on the same type of scale.

Listening

During its history, *Moonlight on a Spring River* has had a number of different titles and versions. It originated as a pipa (lute) piece during the Ching dynasty (1644–1911), and was first entitled 'The sound of the flute and drum in the evening'. It was retitled in 1895, becoming 'Xun Yang' (the name of a river in Shan Xi province). Since 1925 it has usually been an ensemble piece, but is still also played as a pipa solo. It exists in many different versions and instrumentations, like most Chinese tunes.

The version on the CD is an arrangement by Tong Leung-Tak, and is an example of a very old ensemble tradition known as Jiangnan si-zhu. This tradition uses a small ensemble of instruments with mixed and varied timbres – for instance, there may be a bowed string instrument, a plucked string instrument, a flute, and a double-reed instrument. In its melody, the piece makes characteristic use of rising and falling sliding sounds, rather like the tones of the Chinese spoken language. You will notice the pipa being used a great deal here as a solo instrument, accompanied by a variety of other instruments: flute, bowed and plucked string instruments. The intention is not to achieve a homogeneous blend, but to be as expressive as possible, with each player creating a unique line and sound.

Responding

1 Compose a piece called *Moonlight* for wordless voices and one other melodic instrument, e.g. a flute or clarinet. For part of the time give the voices and wind instrument the same line, in unison or octaves. At other times give them separate solo lines. Give the piece an introduction and a short coda.

2 Compose a piece consisting of just a tune, shared by three or four instruments. Give the piece quite a free introduction, and an ending.

3 Listen to more Chinese music, for instance the CD *Like Waves against the Sand* (Saydisc SDL 325), which contains a number of contrasting pieces and styles.

Dance

Based on the *Kecak* dance from Bali

Dance for Wood and Metal

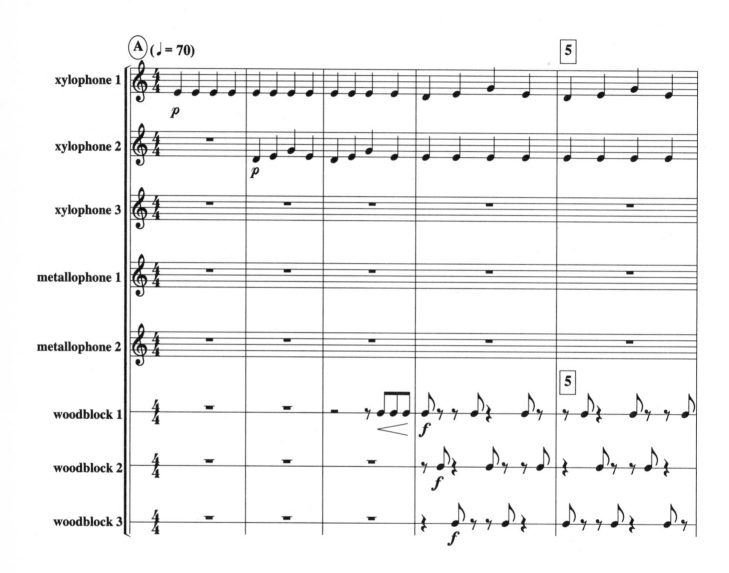

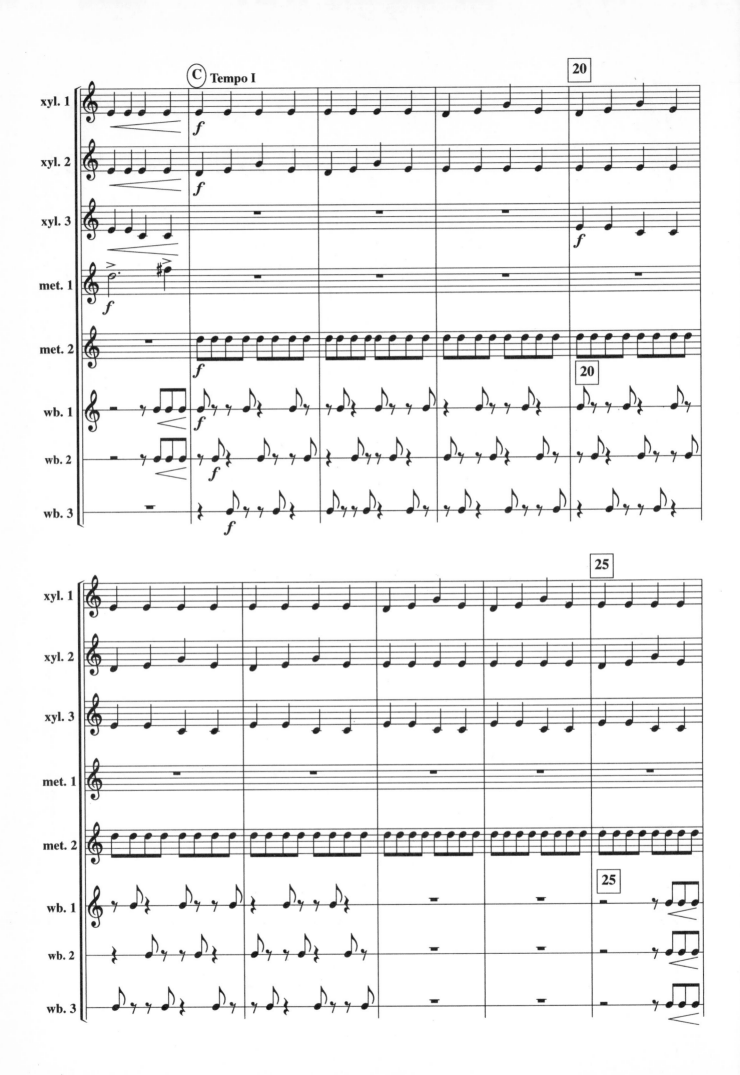

Performing *Dance for Wood and Metal*

The piece is scored for 3 xylophones, 2 metallophones and 3 woodblocks. If these instruments are not available, suitable substitutes may be used – for instance, electronic keyboards with suitable voice-settings. It could also be very exciting to make a vocal version of the piece, and this would make an interesting comparison with the vocal music of the *Kecak* dance.

A conductor is needed, at least for rehearsal. The piece is in $\frac{4}{4}$ time throughout, and it is important that all the players keep absolutely together. Section A is at a moderate tempo (c. ♩=70). Section B should be *suddenly* slower (c. ♩=40), followed by a gradual accelerando back to the original tempo for section C, maintained through section D. There should be no slowing at the end.

The woodblocks play a recurring refrain, which should always be loud but also accurate. It is difficult, and needs careful – preferably separate – rehearsal at a slow tempo.

All the marked dynamics should be observed as closely as possible, with care taken to balance the parts. The woodblock refrain should cut through the texture when it appears.

Analysis and connections

Dance for Wood and Metal

There are three main elements in the piece. The first belongs to the xylophones. Their role is to mark the beat in crotchets. They use only a few notes, grouped around the main note E:

The second element belongs to the metallophones. They add extra interest to the music by entering from time to time with new patterns. For example:

These patterns usually have an effect upon the main beat, either by cutting across it or by dividing it into faster notes. The notes of the metallophones, D and F♯, conflict a little with those of the xylophones, which are grouped around E.

The third element, belonging to the woodblocks, is perhaps the most important. This is the refrain, and it uses a *hocket* technique, so that each player has a quaver at a time. The rhythm of the three woodblocks, 'added

together' and placed on a single line, looks simply like this:

The refrain enters three times, loud and assertive each time. At the last appearance, it is immediately repeated to give the ending extra impetus.

The ending is also notable for being the only passage in the piece where all the instruments are playing at once.

The tempo plan could be represented as follows:

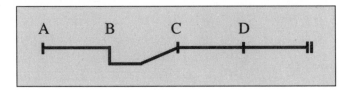

As you can see, there is a sudden change of gear, and then a gradual acceleration.

The Balinese *Kecak* dance

This music is entirely vocal. It has a very noticeable refrain, using the chant 'tjak' repeated very rapidly.

The complete *Kecak* dance contains eight sections, but this recording is of part of the Prologue and second section only. In the Prologue, the *Kecak* ensemble enters and sits in a circle. A prayer is said, and a priest sprinkles holy water on the participants in order to ensure a safe performance. Then the leader calls out (this is the point at which our recorded extract starts) and the performance proper begins. Section 2 commences with the entrance of King Rama and his wife Sita. One day in the forest, Sita finds a golden deer and asks Rama to catch it. He disappears while chasing the deer. . .

While listening, pick out as many as you can of the following features:
- the refrain, used complete and in part
- the use of drones and ostinato patterns
- punctuating sounds
- speech
- slower music for solo voices
- the telling of the story
- sudden changes of speed, accelerandos

Connections

1 Compare the refrains. The *Kecak* refrain is faster and sounds more complicated, but it uses the same techniques as the *Dance for Wood and Metal* refrain. The latter is like a slowed-down version of the former.

2 Both pieces use sudden switches in tempo, and accelerandos.

3 Both use drones, and sounds that mark the pulse (beat).

4 Both use patterns made out of a few notes grouped closely in pitch.

Dance for Wood and Metal is an instrumental piece, and *Kecak* uses voices, but it does so in an instrumental sort of way, in imitation of the Balinese instrumental ensemble, the gamelan.

Listening

Kecak is from the southern part of the Indonesian island of Bali. It was originally an accompaniment to an ancient trance dance, a religious ritual called *sang hyang*, to which a circle of men sang the accompaniment. *Sang hyang* was a ritual designed to protect a village from black magic and disease.

In the early twentieth century *Kecak* became an almost theatrical form, containing episodes from the legendary story *The Ramayana*, in which monkey hordes assist King Rama in battle against the evil King Rawana. The *Kecak* dance is used during the performance of the story.

In *Kecak*, the voices imitate the Balinese gamelan, an ensemble mainly of tuned percussion instruments.

Onomatopoeic sounds are used to impersonate the different instrumental groups, while the 'tjak..., tjak, tjak, tjak' of the refrain represents the monkey hordes.

It is this recurring refrain, with its interlocking rhythm, which is the most striking characteristic of *Kecak*. The voices use a 'hocket' technique, with each voice part contributing a note at a time. The result is a completely regular stream of notes.

Responding

1 Listen to some more Indonesian music, particularly some gamelan. A gamelan is a type of orchestra containing sets of tuned gongs, gong-chimes, metallophones, drums, flutes, bowed and plucked strings, xylophone, small cymbals and singers. The name, derived from two Javanese words, originally meant 'to handle bronze'.

2 Make up a piece for voices using onomatopoeic sounds, for example:

CLICK   CLATTER   CRASH

3 Compose a piece for percussion ensemble, using a recurring refrain. In one section, suddenly have a slower tempo and then get gradually faster.

Kecak dance

Laudate

Based on *Laudate Dominum* for tenor and continuo
by Monteverdi (1567–1643)

Song of Praise

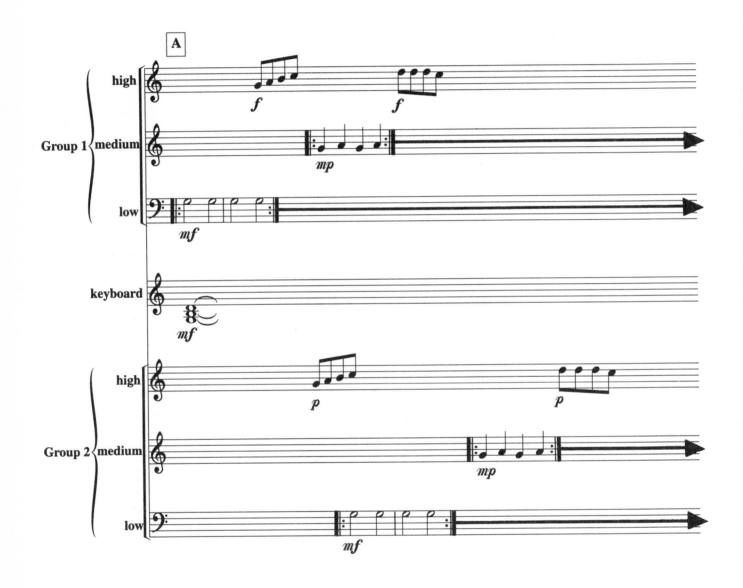

short break

B Quick

hold throughout section

Performing *Song of Praise*

This piece is scored for tuned percussion and one electronic keyboard. The percussion are organised into two separate groups, each with high, medium and low instruments. Groups of string or wind instruments may be used instead of percussion.

It suits the character of the music if the two groups are separated spatially, with the keyboard in the middle:

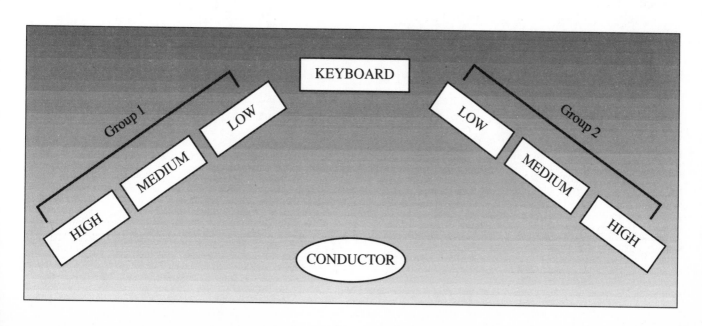

A conductor is essential. His or her role will be:
1 to indicate all the entries in section A,
2 to beat 6 in the last bar of A (which is a $\frac{3}{2}$ bar, but best conducted in 6 rather than 3),
3 to beat a quick $\frac{3}{4}$ through section B, and a slower $\frac{4}{4}$ through section C, with a ritardando at the end.

In section A the tempo should generally be about ♩ = 70, but the parts are not co-ordinated with each other, and the conductor needs to judge the entry of each part by listening and following the score. In section B the tempo should be around ♩ = 100, and in section C around ♩ = 50.

The dynamics are important; *p* must be clearly contrasted with *f*, and *mp* with *mf*, since the echo effects are central to the style.

It is also important that the musical ideas are performed rhythmically.

Analysis and connections

Song of Praise

This piece aims to exploit the idea of musical figures being imitated and echoed across space by two ensembles.

The key is G major, and the harmony is held together by the keyboard part's sustained chords: tonic followed by dominant in section A; alternating tonic and dominant in section B; and tonic in section C with a dominant-to-tonic (V to I) final cadence. The harmony is simple throughout, using only tonic (G) and dominant (D) chords. This helps the decorating flourishes of the upper instruments to be more effective.

The three sections contrast in character. Section A is like an opening flourish or fanfare, with ideas being thrown from the first ensemble to the second and back. It is notated rather freely, without a sense of overall beat until the last bar, which is in $\frac{3}{2}$ time. Section B is in quick triple time, with a dance-like character, and the same sort of imitation and echo between ensembles. Section C is the final flourish, slower than the rest, in strict $\frac{4}{4}$ time, and with an appropriate slowing down at the end.

Monteverdi: *Laudate Dominum*

This music is also in G, though based on an older modal scale. It is written for tenor voice with continuo accompaniment (e.g. organ and cello), and is a setting of one of the Psalms.

The word *laudate* (meaning 'praise') is given special attention by the composer. Near the beginning he uses the notes of the major triad to create a melodic line, and this effective use of simple material is characteristic of his style:

After a very brief slow introduction, the first main section is in fast triple time, quite dance-like in character. It makes much use of the G major triad, of vocal decoration, and also of repeating bass-patterns such as the following:

The second section is slow, with many long notes in the voice part. These are decorated with rapid figures, one-note tremolos, and trills. A feature is the repeated setting of the word *Alleluia*, using rhythms which aptly fit the word:

A brief coda rounds off the piece with two particularly striking vocal phrases (which the singer decorates):

Although notated, the tenor line throughout the piece has the character of free improvisation and spontaneity, with the continuo providing a secure and effective harmonic foundation for the tenor's expressiveness.

The composer sets the words very effectively, with ideas appropriate to particular phrases in the text. For instance:

Listen also for his expressive decoration of the phrase 'in tympano' ('with tambourine'):

in tym - pa - no,
(with tambourine)

Connections

1 Both pieces use the G major triad to create melodic material.
2 Both have a simple harmonic design using only a few chords.
3 The musical figures in both are often brief and simply constructed.
4 The two pieces have a similar overall design:
    slow   faster (in triple time)   slow
5 Both conclude with a final flourish.
6 They both have the same kind of character: robust and declamatory, often like a fanfare. They share an improvisatory character, especially the first section of *Song of Praise* and the last section of Monteverdi's piece.
7 Both make use of a continuo accompaniment to underpin the harmony.

Listening

Claudio Monteverdi (1567–1643) worked for thirty years in Venice, from 1613. His solo motet *Laudate Dominum* was published in 1640 as part of a collection of pieces. It is written in a style which the composer called *stile concitato* or 'agitated style' – a style rich in imitation trumpet calls, repeated bass patterns and vocal decorations. As always in Monteverdi's music, the words are set with great power and authority, and the richly decorated vocal lines are always effective.

The words translate as follows:
    Praise the Lord.
    Praise the Lord in his sanctuary.
    Praise him in his mighty heavens.
    Praise him with the sound of the trumpet,
    Praise him with the harp and lyre,
    Praise him with tambourine and with dance,
    Praise him with clashing cymbals,
    Praise him with resounding cymbals.
    Let everything that breathes praise the Lord.
    Alleluia.

Responding

1 Listen to the spatial and dynamic effects in some more music from seventeenth-century Venice: Giovanni Gabrieli, *In ecclesiis* for solo voices, double chorus and instruments, and *Sonata pian' e forte* for two instrumental groups. And from Monteverdi himself, part of the Vespers of 1610 – *Vespro della Beata Vergine*.
2 Compose a piece for two groups which exploits the spatial positioning of the musicians by having one group of musicians in one position in the room and the other group in a different position.
3 Form two ensembles of equal numbers of players and improvise on the following musical ideas, using imitation, echo, and variation:

Record your improvisations and listen to them. Go a stage further and compose a piece out of the ideas.
4 Listen to Stravinsky's musical setting of almost the same text in the third movement of his *Symphony of Psalms*. Compare his approach to the words with Monteverdi's.

Tune and accompaniment

Based on the first section of Prelude No. 15 in D♭ major
by Chopin (1810–1849)

Prelude for One and Others

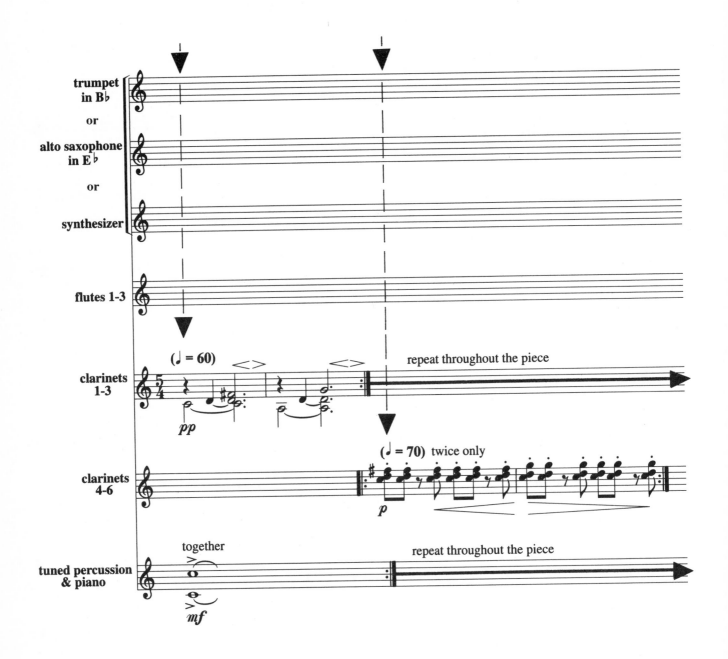

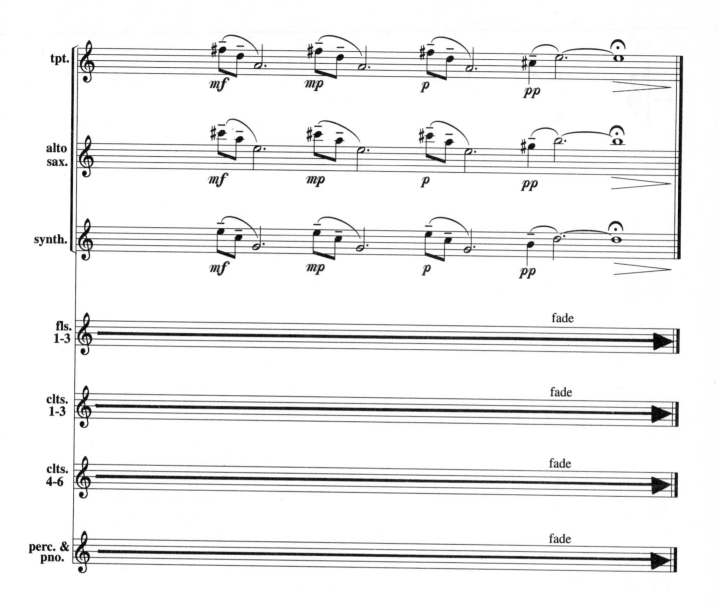

Performing *Prelude for One and Others*

This piece is scored so that it can be used by an instrumental teacher with a whole group. The instrumentation is:

- a solo instrument (trumpet, synthesiser, alto saxophone, or suitable substitute)
- flutes 1–3 (alternatively strings)
- clarinets 1–3 (alternatively strings)
- clarinets 4–6 (alternatively strings)
- tuned percussion and piano

The piece needs a conductor because so much of it is written in free time. The black arrows indicate conductor's signals, the timing of which needs to be judged carefully by following the score and listening.

The role of the solo instrument is very important: once it has started playing, the conductor should take the timing from it. The solo line should be played at about ♩ = 60, with plenty of space left between phrases.

Careful rehearsal of the repeating mobile figures is also important. Clarinets 1–3 need to play at about ♩ = 60, clarinets 4–6 a little faster at ♩ = 70, and similarly for the flutes. The piano and percussion part should be played with the instruments co-ordinated throughout; in fact, within all the parts the players must keep together, even if additional players are used.

The marked dynamics should be followed as accurately as possible, making sure that the solo line is not obscured by the accompaniment figures.

Analysis and connections

Prelude for One and Others

This piece consists basically of a tune and these two accompanying ideas:

The first pattern is played by clarinets 1–3, the second by clarinets 4–6 and later the flutes. These ideas are held together by a pedal-note C on piano and percussion.

The tune floats freely on top of the accompanying figures. It is constructed using the following modal scale, with C as the main note:

It begins with this falling motif:

and then moves away, but returns to the falling motif towards the end – a kind of ABA structure.

Chopin: Prelude No. 15 in D♭ major

Like our performance piece, the texture of this Chopin prelude, which is for solo piano, is tune plus accompaniment. The tune appears in the singing register of the right hand for much of the piece.

The overall structure is ABA with a coda. Section A has the tune in the right hand and the accompaniment in the left, and is in the key of D♭ major. The middle section presents a direct contrast, with the key changing quite suddenly to C♯ minor and the character of the music becoming much more dramatic. Here the focus of the music moves to the lower-pitched area of the left hand and gradually rises until the section reaches its strongest moment. Then the whole process is repeated before a quick change of key returns the music to D♭ major and a recapitulation of the A section's tune. In the coda the tune reaches a high point in pitch, before coming down as the music slows to the end:

One of the most noticeable features of the piece is the way in which the note A♭ (or G♯, as it becomes in the middle section) is present as a quaver pedal note in the accompaniment in almost every bar. For instance, at the very beginning:

And at the beginning of the middle section:

Connections

1 Both tunes start with the same falling motif (though with a slightly different rhythm), and in fact the tune of *Prelude for One and Others* follows closely the contour of Chopin's tune (which is shown below in C major, for ease of comparison):

2 The accompaniment patterns are also related:

3 Both pieces feature a constantly-repeated pedal note in the middle register.

Listening

Chopin's Prelude in D♭ major is nicknamed 'The Raindrop', probably because the persistent A♭ quavers seem to sound like dripping water. However, this was not Chopin's title; he hardly ever attached stories or pictures to his works, but was content to allow the music to speak for itself.

The title 'prelude' originally meant an introductory piece, but by Chopin's time it was regularly used as a title for an independent piece. The Prelude in D♭ major is No. 15 in Chopin's collection of 24 Preludes, Opus 28, composed between 1836 and 1839.

Responding

1 Listen to some of the other Chopin Preludes, for instance the famous ones in A major (No. 7) and C minor (No. 20).

2 Improvise an introduction to *Prelude for One and Others*, in free time, using this set of notes (from which the accompaniment patterns have been built):

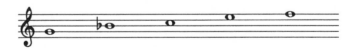

3 Then compose a contrasting middle section, using the following ideas:

Perform the whole piece as a complete A B A structure.

Remember...

When performing...

1 Often exaggerate louds and softs, crescendos and diminuendos.

2 Listen to the other musicians in the piece. This will help you to perform better.

3 Also, listen very carefully to yourself. It is easy to forget to do this.

4 Make sure you can see the conductor.

5 Try to feel the rhythms of the music and articulate them in sound.

6 Don't be nervous about attacking the beginnings of the sounds with energy.

7 In your performing, show a **commitment** to the music.

8 Above all, try to enjoy performing.

When listening...

1 Sometimes listen with maximum concentration for a short time.

2 Sometimes do the opposite – allow the music to wash through you.

3 It can be useful to concentrate on just one element in the music at a time – for example, the rhythms.

4 Get into the habit of listening to music often, but for short periods.

5 Don't 'switch off' because you do not immediately like the music; give it more than one chance to make an impression on you.

CD contents

The listening pieces
TRACK

1. Guillaume de Machaut: the first two sections of the rondeau *Ma fin est mon commencement*
2. Luciano Berio:'O King', the second movement of *Sinfonia*
3. Charles Ives: 'The Housatonic at Stockbridge', No. 3 of *Three Places in New England*
4. Harrison Birtwistle: *Carmen Arcadiae Mechanicae Perpetuum*
5. Judith Weir: 'Bonnie James Campbell' from *Scotch Minstrelsy*
6. John Adams: 'Shaking and Trembling', the first movement of *Shaker Loops*
7. *Moonlight on a Spring River* (Chinese traditional)
8. part of the *Kecak* dance from Bali
9. Claudio Monteverdi: *Laudate Dominum* for tenor and continuo

The performance pieces (all by John Howard)

10. Beethoven Bits
11. Forwards & Backwards
12. Four-part Invention
13. Sang Red
14. River
15. Mechanisms
16. Ballad
17. Loops (version for ensemble)
18. Loops (version for electronic keyboards)
19. Light on the Water
20. Dance for Wood and Metal
21. Song of Praise
22. Prelude for One and Others